Merry Christmas 05

And many more—
love
gg u-m

05

AMERICAN COUNTRY
CHRISTMAS

Clarkson N. Potter, Inc./Publishers

AMERICAN COUNTRY
CHRISTMAS

BY MARY EMMERLING
AND CHRIS MEAD

DESIGN BY JOE CHAPMAN

To Samantha and Jonathan
who have made every Christmas eve
and Christmas morning a joy!
M.E.

To my family and friends,
for all the wonderful Christmases
we've spent together.
C.M.

Copyright © 1989 by Chris Mead, Inc.
Photographs copyright © 1989 by Chris Mead

Published by Clarkson N. Potter, Inc., distributed by Crown Publishers, Inc.,
201 East 50th Street, New York, New York 10022

CLARKSON N. POTTER, POTTER and colophon are trademarks of Clarkson N. Potter, Inc.

Manufactured in Japan

Library of Congress Cataloging-in-Publication Data

Emmerling, Mary Ellisor.
[American country Christmas]
American country Christmas/by Mary Emmerling and Chris Mead; design by Joe Chapman.
1. Christmas—United States. I. Mead, Chris
II. Title. III. Title: American country Christmas.
GT4986.A1E47 1989
394.2'68282—dc20
89-3946
CIP

ISBN 0-517-57386-5

10 9 8 7 6 5 4 3 2 1

First Edition

In the first few weeks of December, when the weather turns cold and shop windows sparkle with holiday decorations, I begin to feel the pleasurable anticipation that makes the Christmas season so special. It's my favorite time of the year, a season filled with unexpected delights that bring out the child in me.

Certain smells, sights, and sounds always evoke memories of my childhood in Georgetown. I remember the warm feeling of sitting at fireside, roasting chestnuts with family and friends; the warm glow of the fire, the smell of the woodsmoke, the lilting aroma of mulled cider and hot buttered rum, and the nostalgic sound of Christmas carols playing on the radio. And of course there was always the wonderful fragrance of the fresh-cut Christmas tree, all aglow with its ornaments and lights. From out the window I could see the soft glow of the moon reflected on the snow-blanketed houses, turning each one into an island of holiday cheer. I loved seeing how each family would decorate their home for the holiday; surprises seemed to be around every corner.

Now that I have a family of my own, I've come to appreciate Christmas as a time of family renewal. My children and I spend special moments together, choosing a Christmas tree and thinking about how we'll decorate it with the ornaments we have collected over the years. I love to fill the house with the soft glow of candles and garlands of greenery for the doors and windows. We fill beloved antique bowls with fruits and nuts, and line the mantel with treasured mememtos of Christmases past. Unpacking the Christmas decorations is a time for me to share my childhood memories with Samantha and Jonathan and to create Christmas memories of our own, like the time we ate all the popcorn before we could string it for the tree. And we have great fun making those melt-in-your-mouth sugar cookies in all the traditional shapes: angels, trees, bells, and Santas. We laugh and hug as we remember these good times—the cookies and milk we always leave for Santa, which are mysteriously gone in the morning—and think happily of the wonderful days still to come.

These weeks before Christmas are a time when smiles betray the secret delight over presents bought and hidden away for loved ones: anything pink and covered with hearts for one friend, a child's storybook—old or new—for another who treasures them, an antique cake stand for still another. The challenge of finding something new and interesting gives me almost as much pleasure as knowing the joy the gifts will bring to their recipients. Anticipation grows as the day draws near, and we all seem filled to the brim with good cheer and fun.

I come from a long line of Christmas traditionalists: my great-great-grandfather, President Benjamin Harrison, had this to say during his second year in office:

We shall have an old-fashioned Christmas tree for the grandchildren upstairs; and I shall be their Santa Claus myself. If my influence goes for aught, let me hope that my example may be followed in every family in the land.

What Grandfather Harrison said in 1891 still calls to me today. Whether we spend Christmas in the bustling city or in the tranquil country, we all long to honor the traditions of Christmas, to gather our families close around us. For Christmas has become a universal celebration: of love of family, of respect for tradition, and of the hope that we all can live in peace. And that is my wish to you!

From Chris Mead and me, happy American Country Christmas,

Mary Emmerling

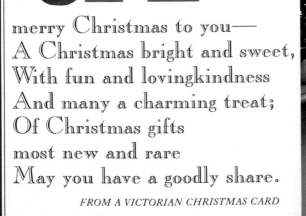

A
merry Christmas to you—
A Christmas bright and sweet,
With fun and lovingkindness
And many a charming treat;
Of Christmas gifts
most new and rare
May you have a goodly share.

FROM A VICTORIAN CHRISTMAS CARD

J

olly old Saint Nicholas,
Lean your ear this way!
Don't you tell a single soul
What I'm going to say;
Christmas Eve is coming soon;
Now you dear old man,
Whisper what you'll bring to me;
Tell me if you can.

TRADITIONAL

Now all our
neighbours' chimneys smoke,
And Christmas blocks
are burning;
Their ovens they with
bakemeats choke,
And all their spits
are turning.
Without the door
let sorrow lie,
And if for cold
it hap to die,
We'll bury it in
a Christmas pie,
And ever more be merry.

GEORGE WITHER

S

ing sweet as the flute
Sing clear as the horn,
Sing joy for the children
Come Christmas morn.

HARRY AND ELEANOR FARJEON

Christmas is coming,
the geese are getting fat,
Please to put a penny
in the old man's hat;
If you haven't got a penny,
a ha'penny will do,
If you haven't got a ha'penny,
then God bless you!

BEGGAR'S RHYME

At
Christmas play
and make good cheer,
For Christmas comes
but once a year.

THOMAS TUSSER

I will honor Christmas in my heart, and try to keep it all the year.

CHARLES DICKENS

The
Christmas day is dawning;
Our carols now we sing;
And pray the coming season
May peacc and gladness bring.

To every one, and all of yours,
We wish a merry day,
And hope some of its pleasures
Through all the year may stay.

L. A. FRANCE

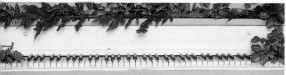

Before

these stood the two Yule candles beaming like two stars of the first magnitude; other lights were distributed in branches, and the whole array glittered like a firmament of silver.

WASHINGTON IRVING

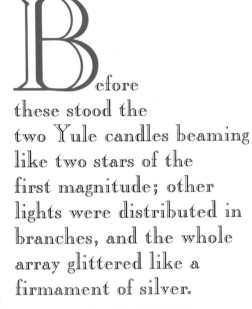

H

eap on more wood!
—the wind is chill;
But let it whistle
as it will,
We'll keep our
Christmas
merry still.

SIR WALTER SCOTT

I'll hang up my stocking
to hold what he brings;
I hope he will fill it
with lots of nice things:
He <u>must</u> know how dearly
I love sugar plums;
I'd like a big box
when Santa Claus comes.

ELIZABETH SILE

Whence

Santa Claus comes,
or whither he goes,
Is something, dear Tommy,
that nobody knows.
We know that the best of
magicians is he,
And vainly we guess how
such wonders can be;
But one thing is certain,
he's here and away,
To cheer all the children
and brighten the day.

ANONYMOUS

Twas
the night before Christmas,
when all through the house,
Not a creature was stirring,
not even a mouse;
The stockings were hung
by the chimney with care,
In hopes that Saint Nicholas
soon would be there.

CLEMENT C. MOORE

I heard the bells
on Christmas Day
Their old familiar
carols play,
And wild and sweet
The word repeat
Of peace on earth,
good-will to men!

HENRY WADSWORTH LONGFELLOW

N ow

is the season of the
holly and the mistletoe;
the days are come
in which we hang
our rooms with
the sober green of
December and feel it
summer in our hearts.

SATURDAY EVENING POST,
DECEMBER 29, 1866

L

ittle Jack Horner
sat in the corner,
Eating a Christmas pie:
He put in his thumb,
and pulled out a plum,
And said "What a
good boy am I!"

NURSERY RHYME

S
well the notes
of Christmas song!
Sound it forth through
the earth abroad!

FRANCES RIDLEY HAVERGAL

O Christmas tree,
O Christmas tree,
How true you stand unchanging.

TRADITIONAL GERMAN FOLK SONG

Villagers all,
this frosty tide,
Let your doors
swing open wide
Though wind
may follow and
snow betide
Yet draw us in
by your fire
to bide:
Joy shall be
yours in the
morning.

KENNETH GRAHAME

My best of wishes for your merry Christmases and your happy New Years, your long lives and your true prosperities. Worth twenty pound good if they are delivered as I send them. Remember? Here's a final prescription added, "To be taken for life."

CHARLES DICKENS

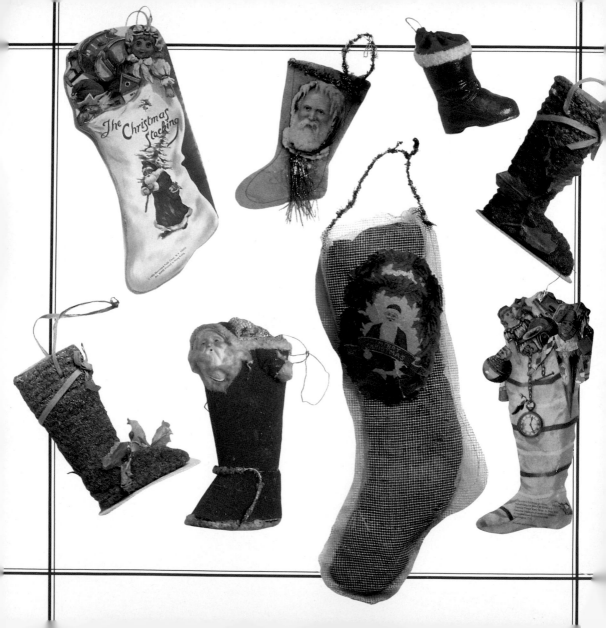

Green grow'th the holly,
So doth the ivy;
Though winter blasts
blow ne'er so high,
Green grow'th the holly.

SIXTEENTH-CENTURY ENGLISH VERSE

Christmas is here:
Winds whistle shrill,
Icy and chill.
Little care we;
Little we fear
Weather without,
Sheltered about
The Mahogany Tree.

WILLIAM MAKEPEACE THACKERAY

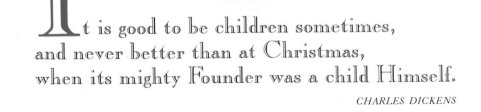

It is good to be children sometimes,
and never better than at Christmas,
when its mighty Founder was a child Himself.

CHARLES DICKENS

SPECIAL THANKS TO:
PAM KRAUSS; BARBARA TRUJILLO; MARILYN HANNIGAN;
BOB AND SUE EDEN; MARSTON LUCE; EVE WILSON;
SUSAN AND TONY VICTORIA; ELIZABETH GERSCHALL;
MORGAN AND GERRI MACWHINNIE; BARBARA JOHNSON;
FOX TAVERN; DON KELLY AND WARREN FITZSIMMONS;
BARBARA STRAWSER; PAT RANALLO; PINE CONE ANTIQUES;
JIMMY CRAMER AND DEAN JOHNSON;
SUZANNE AND TRAVIS WORSHAM; MARIE PLUMMER GOETT;
JOHN C. NEWCOMER AND BETTY PHILLIPS;
PAT HOLMES; AUDREY JULIAN; GOTHAM BOOK MART;
NANCY THOMAS; EAST HAMPTON HISTORICAL SOCIETY;
CAROL PFLUMM; TODDY GOODSPEED; JOE CHAPMAN;
AND EVERYONE AT CLARKSON N. POTTER.